DON'T GO FOR HOME RUNS, SINGLES WILL DO

TACTICAL INVESTMENT FOR WEALTH CREATION IN RETIREMENT

PATRICK DELANEY

Don't Go for Home Runs, Singles Will Do
Copyright © 2020 by Patrick Delaney

All rights reserved. No part of this publication may be reproduced, distributed, or transmitted in any form or by any means, including photocopying, recording, or other electronic or mechanical methods, without the prior written permission of the author, except in the case of brief quotations embodied in critical reviews and certain other non-commercial uses permitted by copyright law.

Tellwell Talent
www.tellwell.ca

ISBN
978-0-2288-4267-5 (Paperback)
978-0-2288-4268-2 (eBook)

Dedications

This book is dedicated to the memory or our youngest son Patrick Jr, who was killed in a car accident at age 21. We'll see you soon son. We love and miss you.

Acknowledgements

First I'd like to commend my editor Graham Browning who made my words read much better - I'd go as far as saying "smooth as silk". His financial background, experience and work were invaluable to making this book a reality. Thank you so much Graham.

I'd like to also thank Doug Roy (my friend of 58 years) and Gerry Walsh (my U. S. friend from my days at Oxy) who both read over my "draft manuscript" and offered many valuable suggestions; each from different perspectives. Thanks guys!

I'd like to thank my sons Kevin and David. Kevin - who used this dividend stock path successfully and retired early - and David, who not only used the same dividend approach but also financed his mortgage with his RSP, as described in my book. His past experience has helped me immeasurably. Their continued support from start to finish was very important to me.

Finally to my wife of 57 years Helen, who has always been there for me. Together we weathered some troubled times and remained standing. Her values and common sense have been ingrained in all of our family. It'll always be her forever.

Table of Contents

Dedications.. iii

Acknowledgements..v

Chapter 1: Embarking on my DIY investment journey.........1

Chapter 2: Will I run out of money before I run out of life?... 5

Chapter 3: The financial perils of mutual funds 9

Chapter 4: The Halloween Massacre
(taxing income trusts) 13

Chapter 5: The RSP trap...16

Chapter 6: Navigating the WebBroker trading platform.....19

Chapter 7: Unintended and purposely created capital losses.....24

Chapter 8: Compounding TFSA contributions
by dividend swapping..28

Chapter 9: Tracking net worth and predicting
annual income...32

Chapter 10: Beefing up income by dividend and bank
hopping..37

Chapter 11: RSP mortgages 41

Chapter 12: My portfolio and how I get my money 44

Chapter 13: The good and bad lessons learned on my journey....47

Afterword...51

A Glossary of Terms...53

Chapter 1

EMBARKING ON MY DIY INVESTMENT JOURNEY

Everybody out there has a story to tell. Some people are knowledgeable about world events and others ignore them. Some are aware of their finances and others just live for today and will worry about tomorrow later. Some budget, save and don't go into debt, while others say "the hell with it, let the government look after me when I retire". There are some who spend more time planning for their vacations than for their retirement. Some live modest lifestyles, are not flashy or ostentatious and are content to put their savings in GICs. But everybody has a story to tell about their life experiences and why it turned out like it did.

We've all heard that you need to invest a million dollars (or some such figure) – with an experienced advisor to show you the way – to fund your retirement. I found out differently: you can DIY even though you have no experience in investing. In this book I've provided a pathway which has worked for me that you might consider. So here's my journey; the lessons I've learned by trial and error and my footsteps to follow to achieve a comfortable retirement lifestyle.

At age 82, I've written this for the benefit of other **would-be retirees** who are trying to work out if they can leave the workforce. I've been down that road, starting at rock bottom in financial investing knowledge, knowing nothing and wondering what to do. Should I seek the paid help of an advisor? Could I do it myself? That's what I was faced with when I left the workforce in 1996, 24 years ago.

Some of the strategies I have used or developed can be applied by **anybody** of any age and level of experience who wants to invest in the market and make money. Chapters 7, 8, 9, 10, 11 and 12 might be more applicable to **experienced** investors. It would be a shame to croak without sharing these techniques!

I started with modest savings in GICs and did everything myself. Instead of just living on those savings and running out of money at the age of 84 (my actuarial lifespan when I quit my job in 1996), my wife and I have saved tens of thousands of dollars in taxes and advisor fees by doing it my way. Despite using our savings extensively for living expenses, I was able to **triple** our initial original investment to leave as our legacy.

Here's the **roadmap** of what I did, what I discovered along the way and how I've ended up. You might use the stock trading and tax-advantaged strategies I've developed yourself.

Described herein are things I've found as I went from seeking "free" advice from financial experts, buying mutual funds, transitioning into income trusts and finally investing in dividend-paying stocks that I selected and can "live with". What I've found out, **you can do too**; here's how.

Don't Go for Home Runs, Singles Will Do

***

I graduated from high school at Stamford Collegiate in 1957, and to make money for school I spent a year working in the control laboratory at Cyanamid of Canada in Niagara Falls, Ontario. In the spring of 1958, I wrote an entry IQ test and was accepted into what was then a new concept for Canadian universities; an engineering co-op program. This program alternated classroom learning with working in industry, which in my case was at Cyanamid. I was one of the first 75 engineering graduates from the University of Waterloo in 1962; I was a chemical engineer.

I started working full-time at Cyanamid in 1962, got married in 1963 and in 1966 I got a job in the corporate engineering department of Hooker Chemical in Niagara Falls, New York. In 1967, Occidental Petroleum acquired Hooker and we became their corporate engineering department. My three sons were born while I worked at Oxy; in 1967, 1969 and 1972. I developed mathematical computer simulations used as an aid in process design, process optimization and computer control; it was a dream job. In the severe recession of 1982 I was laid off along with 70% of the corporate engineering department. The department was eventually dissolved over the next few years after moving to Houston, Texas.

I spent more than a year consulting and teaching part-time at college and university, and in 1983 I got a full-time position teaching computer programming, math, accounting and management at Niagara College in Niagara Falls, Ontario. In 1996, two years after the loss of our youngest son, I found it too difficult to continue so I left the workforce at age 58, seven years before my normal retirement age of 65; despite taking a 21% reduction on my teaching pension. Thus, I began the third career of my working life: that of financial investing, and the topic of this book.

During my engineering and teaching careers, the only investments I had the time or inclination to make were five-year GICs. This time frame spanned inflationary periods when mortgage rates were around 20%, as were the returns for GICs and the now extinct Canada Savings Bonds. Since I commuted to work each day in the United States, I wasn't eligible to contribute to an RSP, so all our savings were in after-tax money. While I knew nothing about the stock market then, I do remember the Dow Jones index was at about 1,000 in the early 1980s. At the time of writing (July–August 2020), it's above 27,000. But there's another scary U.S. election coming!

I had struggled with the decision to "retire" from work; could the four of us survive on my Oxy and Niagara College pensions? My wife had always been a home-maker and neither one of us had received an inheritance, which compounded the dilemma. To see if it was possible, I projected all of our cash flows (money in and money out) into the future to determine how much it would cost us to live, using cash from our GICs to top up any shortfalls in my pension incomes.

It seemed daunting; how can you predict into an uncertain future? I would need to know when to draw on my government pensions, and what interest and inflation rates were going to be. But it had to be done! Chapter 2 is the first step in my DIY investing discovery.

Chapter 2

WILL I RUN OUT OF MONEY
BEFORE I RUN OUT OF LIFE?

With our GIC savings, would it be possible to retire early? Excluding big-ticket items, how much does it cost us to live now? That's where I started.

I've had a CIBC checking account for over 65 years and all our bills and expenditures come out of that one account: credit card payments, transfers to other accounts, ATM cash withdrawals, cheques, pre-authorized utility bills, city taxes, transfers to virtual banks and CRA quarterly tax installments all flow from that one account. All our cash inflows go into that account, too: work and government pensions, U.S. Social Security (converted into Canadian money), brokerage dividends, rebate cheques, CRA refunds, etc. I get free monthly transaction statements showing all these inflow and outflows, so determining our monthly cost of living expenses was easy, readily available and accurate. I had kept a record of the average of our annual living expenditures on a spreadsheet for years. I was also able to keep track of big-ticket items, such as a new furnace, A/C, cars, re-roofing and driveway paving.

But these living expenses will rise with inflation. Governments want to maintain a 2% inflation rate for growth and prosperity, so I originally assumed a 2% annual increase in expenses too. The costs of major purchases also rise with inflation.

How long could we expect to live? At age 58, my actuarial life projection indicated that I would live to be 84. So, for my new spreadsheet, I assumed that both my wife and I would live to that age. If I had been 70, my life expectancy might have been about 17 years; if you live longer, apparently you'll continue to live longer.

The next thing was to determine how much our savings could expect to grow over this 26-year period. In 1996, you could put your money in the bank and get 5% interest a year "just by rolling out of bed". High-interest virtual bank accounts (I used ING Direct, now owned by Scotiabank and rebranded as Tangerine) yielded in excess of 5%. So when our five-year GICs came due, they went into ING, where I could get any or all of it back within 24 hours with no charges. Thus, they could be drawn on as needed for living expenses to supplement my pension incomes, and the remainder could draw interest until the next year's top-up came around.

But when would I need to draw on these savings? My spreadsheet showed ages 58 through 90 down the side, and different cash flows across the top. Pension incomes could start at different ages, which I could change if needed. I could start taking CPP at age 60, but my CPP benefit was small. I was only able to contribute to it for 13 years while I was working in Canada, mainly at an entry-level salary from ages 45 to 58. As I rose up the grid, my salary and CPP deductions increased. My CPP

Don't Go for Home Runs, Singles Will Do

benefit would be about $285 per month, which I would split with my wife for tax purposes. She would get a CPP payment of $12 per month; she only made one monthly contribution, in January 1967, before she quit to give birth to our oldest son in April of that year. But she had to split her CPP with me, too! We'd both collect OAS at age 65. My work pensions also started early; the teacher's pension at 60 and I'd already started to take my Oxy pension when I was 56.

Since I had commuted for work in the United States for 17 years, I could apply for U.S. Social Security (SS) at age 62; the earliest possible. But they reduced my SS by the amount of CPP I'd draw! What did that have to do with my U.S. pension? But they said "rules were rules". One notable aside: I remember that my annual SS premium in 1980 was around US$3,200 per year, while my highest maximum CPP contribution was $1,850; a sizeable difference. But my Oxy pension and SS payments were in U.S. dollars and the exchange was in my favour at that time, but again unpredictable; what would it be in the future? While working in the United States I had experienced the dollar exchange both ways.

Another notable aside: while working for Oxy I paid state and federal taxes and then got a tax credit when filing my Canadian taxes. I would convert my U.S. income into Canadian funds, subtract my U.S. tax credit and pay on the difference. My U.S. taxes were high enough to completely negate paying Canadian taxes, except for taxes on any interest I'd made here. U.S. taxes were high because I couldn't file a joint return; for

U.S. tax purposes I was designated as a single man with a wife and children as exemptions.

Entering these data into my spreadsheet – all the cash inflows and outflows, based on different assumptions for inflation, interest and exchange rates – I was able to compute how much I'd have to draw on our ING savings each year to maintain our standard of living. I also made a contingency each year for big-ticket expenditures. Each year after the ING top-up withdrawal, I assumed the remaining savings would increase by what I thought would be the interest rate that year – initially I used a value of 5%. However, some years we needed around 15% of our ING savings for additional living expenses. And interest rates had dropped dramatically too, much lower than I'd expected. Our savings dwindled!

Our standard of living (travel, entertainment, etc.) had dropped and taken a complete change of direction after our family tragedy. While it was modest, it was still very comfortable. But I did show that our savings would likely run out by the age of 84 – wow, that's less than two years from now!

In any case, just using our savings wasn't going to work, so I abandoned this approach and sought other ways. The only other game in the house in the late 1990s was investing in **mutual funds,** which I found out was fraught with danger; fees and commissions would be sapping our money.

Chapter 3

THE FINANCIAL PERILS OF MUTUAL FUNDS

Mutual funds were popular at that time and seemed like a viable option, but I would have to use an advisor – who charged fees – to buy them. I started reading the *Money Reporter* and the *Canadian MoneySaver*, which gave information and advice on different investment vehicles – mutual funds, stocks, bonds, etc. I also subscribed to the *Canadian Mutual Fund Adviser* and I talked with various financial advisors, who charged nothing for an exploratory meeting. One proposed GIC laddering: splitting our savings into five portions and putting them into one, two, three, four and five-year GICs, taking out what I needed each year as each one matured and putting the remainder into new five-year GICs. But as I had already found out, that wouldn't work even with the interest rates available then for GICs.

Most advisors said they'd invest our savings in mutual funds and manage my money for me. They didn't mention specifically they'd get a commission from the company managing the fund they chose for me. Since that seemed like the best idea at the time, I split our savings into three segments; I gave one-third to an advisor to invest for me, one-third I invested myself with a no-commission broker (I believe it was Meloche Monnex) and invested the remaining portion with Phillips, Hager & North (PH&N), an independent company based in Vancouver, where I could choose any of their funds myself. Another notable aside: the DIY Meloche Monnex broker that I had chosen became TD Bank's insurance subsidiary and the brokerage morphed into TD Waterhouse Discount Brokerage (now called TD Direct Investing), while PH&N were acquired by RBC Royal Bank.

I learned that financial advisors (or "salesmen") got paid by the fund company offering the mutual fund they invested in for me, either by an upfront negotiable 5% fee based on the amount of my investment or through a deferred sales charge (DSC). A DSC would take off, say, 6% of my original investment if I redeemed the fund after one year, 5% after two years, and sliding down to zero after six years. That kept you under their fund umbrella. But advisors say buying mutual funds are "free" – with the DSC caveat. PH&N were private then, and required a minimum initial investment of $25,000 to buy into their fund family. They had low management expense ratio (MER) fees – more of which to follow – and their sales people only got paid if their funds were successful. My DIY option charged no fees and had fewer DSC restrictions, but these were still somewhat onerous.

Some fund companies allowed me to move from one of their funds to another under their umbrella – say from energy to blue chip – without triggering a DSC. Most fund companies also had a "money market" fund under their umbrella, so if you moved to that and then redeemed the units, you'd eliminate any DCS. I used this approach to get out of Altimera's funds

I got through Meloche Monnex; at that time, Altimera was a company that managed a family of funds.

I also found out that if you bought a fund late in the year, you might be stuck with capital gains on your taxes because the fund had made capital gains earlier in the year. That would be apportioned to you on your T3, even if your fund subsequently lost value. That's hard to swallow. So buy them early in the year.

Every mutual fund has a MER comprising their operating expenses, management fees, paperwork, research, etc. A typical MER is 2.5% and is taken out of your investment each year – even if your chosen fund yielded nothing. A *Financial Post* columnist once cited the Rule of 40: divide 40 by the MER to show how many years it will take for your investment to lose one-third of its value. For example, 40 divided by a typical MER of 2.5 equals 16; thus, in 16 years you'd only have 67% of whatever you would have had if there was no MER. To prove this to myself, I checked it out with a separate spreadsheet I developed to prove this. PH&N's family of funds all had low MERs, meaning this 33% loss was pushed out further into the future.

Your financial advisor might also charge an annual fee for administering your accounts – on top of the mutual fund company charges – and for giving you investing advice. Also your advisor could only "sell" (redeem) your funds only after 8 pm that day, hampering your inter-day decisions when the market's moving up and down rapidly.

A few years ago it was said that 80% of mutual fund managers couldn't match their stock index benchmark – such as the Dow Jones index, S&P, or TSX, despite their wealth of research and experience. So the move began to just buy the benchmark market index (known as an ETF – exchange-traded fund). There was also a move to reconstruct many mutual funds, changing from stocks in different companies to a family of indexes. This somewhat lowered their MERs too.

Around 2003, I sold all my mutual funds and transitioned them into income trusts. These were very high distribution vehicles and funds that were actually stocks that could bought and sold on the stock market. I opened a trading account with TD Waterhouse Discount Brokerage (now called TD Direct Investing) to administer my accounts with absolutely no fees or charges. And TD Waterhouse (TDW) paid me back for the fees charged by my mutual fund advisors when they closed out my accounts! Whenever I bought or sold a stock it cost me $29.99 – it's now only $9.99 – no matter how many shares I bought or sold. They provided all the tax documentation I needed for filing (T3, T5, T4RIF, etc.), stock analyses, technical investing techniques, trading confirmations and monthly statements – all free. Best thing since sliced bread! I'll cover more about their features later.

I was happily making a good monthly income until the 2006 **Halloween Massacre** came along. That's the subject of the next chapter.

Chapter 4

THE HALLOWEEN MASSACRE (TAXING INCOME TRUSTS)

Income trusts (ICTs) were investment vehicles that didn't pay corporate taxes to the government; they distributed all their free cash flows to their unit holders, who then paid income and capital gains taxes based on their particular tax rate. A normal corporation would have paid 30% of their profits to the government in corporate taxes and used whatever was left for expansion, acquisitions or dividends. Stock holders received a T3 slip showing the distributions they had to declare. With a normal corporation these amounts are increased by about 40% to account for the corporate taxes already paid, and investors are compensated by a dividend tax credit of around 12%. They also issued a T5 for tax filing.

The stock ticker symbols for income trusts are different from normal corporations. For example, the ticker symbol for Scotiabank is BNS, while the income trust Enervest had the symbol EIT.UN; the ".UN" suffix represents units. Whenever you buy or sell a stock, you use their ticker symbol in the process.

The holders of income trust units – who are actually "stock" holders, since the units were purchased on the market – get their taxable distributions reported on T3 slips. These include capital gains, actual dividends, interest income and return of capital; return of capital is discussed later. So I moved all my mutual funds into income trusts for their high distributions. As I had a low taxable income I didn't pay much tax.

From the government's standpoint, they did end up getting their tax money from most unit holders every year, but because some unit holders put their investment into tax-deferred RSPs the government had to wait until the money was withdrawn, years down the road, to get their tax money; not so good for governments who want their money right away. Also, pension funds invested heavily in ICTs, which shielded the profits from taxation until their retirees began drawing their pensions. This wouldn't be taxed for years either.

Income trusts were not interested in expansion either, just in satisfying their unit holders. The Liberals threatened to start taxing ICTs but backed down prior to the 2006 election; which they lost anyway. The Conservatives promised that they would not tax ICTs, but after six months or so they did a 180. On Halloween evening, Finance Minister Jim Flaherty (now deceased) announced they'd start to charge 30% taxes on ICTs after a period of four years. The Conservatives said that ICTs could retain their ICT format for four years but would then start paying 30% taxes, or they could transition into a normal corporate structure paying 30% corporate tax. They claimed Canada's competitive mode would be eroded, apparently triggered by news from BCE Inc. (Bell Canada's holding company), who had signalled they would go to ICT mode too. My investment income dropped by 30% overnight!

I figured that if the government could, at the stroke of a pen, affect my savings so dramatically I had to do something. So I kept all of my existing ICTs for that four-year period but stopped buying new units. I saved whatever distribution money I could and started emergency or "rainy day" savings accounts at ING and President's Choice Bank (another high-interest savings bank that was CIBC's virtual bank at that time). After the four-year period expired, I started investing in dividend-paying stocks, one of which is a carry-over from the old ICT format; EIT.UN, which paid a distribution of over 13%.

EIT.UN is our largest holding. It is very tax efficient and therefore well suited for our taxable non-registered accounts (which I refer to as NRAs). What about my RSP? An RSP is a registered retirement fund that can be used to reduce taxable income by the amount contributed, which is set annually by the government. Thus, RSPs are untaxed money that when withdrawn becomes taxable. What should I put in them? See Chapter 5.

Chapter 5

THE RSP TRAP

Before covering my foray into dividend-paying stocks, I would like to cover a bit of portfolio construction first; specifically my RSPs, which were converted to RIFs when I turned 71. Both my wife (who has a spousal RIF) and I only have cash in our RIFs. Currently they comprise about 10% of our net worth, but we need some stability and to reduce what we have to pay the government in taxes from the mandatory RIF withdrawals. So we have laddered three-year GICs and take out the minimum amount possible; five-year rates are almost identical to the three's. And the RIFs are small compared to our overall savings, as discussed later, so the tax load is not significant.

To convert our RIFs from the stocks they originally contained, I swapped the stocks "in kind" (as whole stocks at market value) with matching cash from our NRAs. This was done with no tax liability at all, since the total monetary value of our RIFs remained the same after the swap as before, just with a different content. Experts said "you can't do that", but I had done it for a several years before the government disallowed the practice. So don't rely solely on experts, find out for yourself. I could have sold the stocks in the RIFs and then re-bought it in our NRAs, but there were stock commissions to pay and buy/sell differences to contend with. In my son's RSP, there were 25-year strip bonds yielding 10% where the buy/sell difference was quite appreciable, and he needed to have cash in his RSP to use for his entire house mortgage (this practice is covered in Chapter 11). But the swapping was nice as long as it lasted!

However, I'd previously bought some dividend stocks in our RIFs as well, some of which I DRIPped (i.e. used a dividend reinvestment plan). For example, you can choose for, say, Scotiabank to convert their quarterly dividend into stock instead of cash for you at no charge. But that must be done when the company chooses, not you; it might be when the price is high and you'd get fewer shares. Also, the amount of the dividend issued must be sufficient to buy whole shares of stock, not fractions of shares. Currently a share is worth about $55, so your dividend has to be large enough to purchase one, two or more whole shares, with the remainder put into your brokerage account as cash.

During the oil boom, when oil reached over $100, I had Trilogy Energy DRIPping their dividend, but when the oil bottomed out, Trilogy's share price dropped too. While this gave me more shares each month, the overall amount of my investment dropped. When it dropped too low I sold. So I learned a lesson: no more DRIPping. Since the charge for buying new shares is only $9.99 now, you can do it yourself whenever you deem it advantageous.

In retrospect, I'm glad I couldn't use RSPs while I was working in the United States and could only contribute small amounts for the 13 years I was teaching in Canada. As I mentioned earlier, since I started at an entry-level salary, contributions were low initially until I moved gradually up the grid to a maximum salary. I would have been sucked into the

RSP trap – because all amounts taken out of an RSP or RIF are taxable! Most of my investments are in after-tax or NRA taxable accounts, so I have far more flexibility over how much tax I pay – and when I pay it; this strategy is covered in more detail in Chapters 7, 8 and 10. That's why advisors always say "everybody is different"; there's no single retirement solution for all. Everybody is unique.

In my TD Direct Investing account (described in detail in Chapter 6) there are six accounts: the taxable NRA, TFSA account and taxable RIF that my wife and I each hold. The RIFs contain GICs with a small spousal variable annuity (Manulife's PensionBuilder). Our NRAs and TFSAs hold dividend-paying stocks. Our TFSAs also contain high-interest savings accounts to temporarily hold our monthly dividend money – more on this later.

As a preview of future chapters – and to keep you interested – I have projected that, as of early July, our annual income for 2020 will be approximately 60% higher than my final Oxy or top-of-the-grid's teacher's salary; **34%** from our government pensions, **18.4%** from my work pensions, **15.5%** from TFSA tax-free dividends, **12.6%** from taxable NRA dividends, **8.3%** from RIFs, **6.9%** anticipated realized capital gains and **4.3%** interest. I keep two spreadsheets: one for showing our annual income from these sources for tax planning and the other to track our net worth (excluding our house); there's more in later chapters covering these spreadsheets.

Now let's look at how I – and you – can easily invest in stocks and keep track of their performance: TD Waterhouse's WebBroker **trading platform**.

Chapter 6

NAVIGATING THE WEBBROKER TRADING PLATFORM

Disclosure: I get no money or favours for this "recommendation" of the TD Direct Investing WebBroker trading platform – but I've used it for many years and I am very satisfied.

As I recollect, to open an account you go to a local TD Bank – after making a phone call appointment – and they'll have you fill in the paperwork. Also, you need the information on all the accounts where your investments currently reside. You'll fill in the paperwork to authorize TDW to transfer those accounts to their platform. Any fees charged by your current financial institutions for their close-out services are taken out of your investments before the transfer but can be pre-negotiated with TDW to be reimbursed to you; unless the amount of your investment is trivial. You'll be notified by regular mail – or these days, more likely by e-mail with an appropriate security system – with your new TD Direct Investing account numbers and a computer login number and temporary password for the WebBroker online trading platform. You can phone their 1-800 number and they'll walk you through all or any part of this preamble during your first login.

You can then log in to WebBroker using that number and temporary password, change it to a "permanent" password of your choice, scan the legal verbiage, click on the boxes to agree and you'll be connected. You'll see their home page. Let's say you have – like I do – your NRA, TFSA, and RIF and your spouse's NRA, TFSA and RIF accounts all along the top. Click on your NRA (remember, that's my acronym, not theirs) and you'll see your money and any securities you've transferred listed under Holdings. Other headings available are Allocations, Activity, Performance, Gains & Losses and Projected Income. For any stock you own, it'll show how many shares you have, what its current price is (in real time), what you paid for it and how much it's up or down. Also shown beside each share is a buy/sell button to add or subtract from your holding – more on trading later. The Activities option opens a page showing the transactions that have been done recently, such as receiving a dividend for different stocks, buying or selling stocks and for how much, any extra deposits made from your local TD Bank (you may have bought more shares and needed the money to complete the purchase) and any withdrawals of money (e.g. dividends or final sale proceeds).

In my case, my dividends from each stock are deposited into the cash portion of my NRA account on the 15th of the month (for EIT.UN), with the exception of quarterly payments (at the end of April, July, October and January) from BNS (Enbridge (ENB) also pays quarterly) – all in cash. I phone TDW's 1-800 number, verify my identity either by prearranged computer voice recognition or by answering questions about information in my accounts. To the TDW representative answering, I say, "Please transfer X dollars from account Y to my CIBC account on record." They repeat my order and after I've confirmed it, it's sent. If this is done before 10 am, it's in my CIBC account that evening; otherwise it'll be there the next day.

If you purchase stocks without having the cash already in your account, you have two days – it used to be three – to make a deposit at your TD Bank branch. It'll be instantaneously transferred into your TD Direct Investing account.

If you want to buy shares in a stock you don't already own, you click on the buy/sell icon at the top of the home page (a circle with up and down arrows). This opens a screen where you can enter the stock ticker symbol for the security you want (e.g. BNS, ENB). You'll also click on how many shares you want. Boxes open up to show the current bid/ask prices for that stock, and how many shares are offered or requested by others. The amount of free cash in your NRA account is also shown. You can select whether you want to buy these shares at the current market price or to limit how much you want to buy it for. Then you set how long your offer is to last.

Next, it'll ask you for a trading password, which you must have already set up. You can preview how much your transaction will cost and how much free cash you will have left in your NRA account after the trade. If it all looks fine, you click OK and it's done. At the top right you can click on the trade status icon (check mark in a circle) and see how much you actually paid for your shares.

For stocks you already own, you can click on the holdings menu and the buy/sell box opposite that stock will show your holdings. The same buy/sell screen will open to show the stock symbol and number of shares you own. You can adjust this number accordingly if you want to buy or sell shares. After that it's just a case of setting market or limit price and entering your trading password again.

Let's say you want to buy a stock that's thinly traded (not many shares bought or sold that day; maybe 2,000 shares). You'll notice there's a big difference between what sellers want to get and how much buyers need to pay to get it. So you might want to put in a buy limit and specify how much you want to pay for it, and a time limit for how long the offer lasts; for example, the rest of the day or for longer? You might ask to buy it below the market price until the end of the day, but you may not get it. I've done both market and limit, sometimes successfully and sometimes not. Sometimes I've kept "chasing" the stock, changing what I wanted to pay all day, but to no avail. Lately I just go with the market price; it's easier.

If the stock's very liquid (many shares being traded; around 100,000 or more) then there's very little difference between the buy and sell price. On the home page, you can click on Accounts and then Document (e-services), where you can then click to view your statements, confirmations, tax documents, corporate actions or delivery preferences.

When buying or selling stocks in a TFSA or RIF you must have the money in the account – for example, your current year's TFSA allowance of $6,000 or your RSP contribution room based on the CRA's assessment of your salary and company pension adjustment – before making the trade.

Transferring money from a TFSA to our CIBC account (in other words, de-registering the cash) must be done by phone. Sending money the other way (into a TFSA) must also be done via phone, and RSP contributions can be made by cheque at your TD Bank branch.

Once a month, TDW provides online statements for your records; how much you have in each account and how many transactions (inflows and outflows) were made during the month. They also provide T3, T5 and T4RIFs for income taxes in the early part of the year. As I mentioned, WebBroker provides the option to view or print out your stock trading confirmations, which may be required for a CRA audit. More on filing taxes will be covered later.

There are many features available on WebBroker that I don't use or need, such as how your stocks are performing, technical stock trading analysis procedures and research tools. You could spend days exploring all these features. And they are all free.

Any problem or concerns I've had have been quickly resolved by phoning the TD Direct Investing helpline or request line (I use 1-800-668-1972). Now let's see what kind of **trading strategies** can be employed, starting in Chapter 7.

Chapter 7

UNINTENDED AND PURPOSELY CREATED CAPITAL LOSSES

At first, I used several sources to choose stocks to buy for our taxable accounts: *Money Reporter*, *Canadian Mutual Fund Adviser* (when we still had mutuals), *Canadian MoneySaver*, the *National Post*'s Financial Post section and BNN Bloomberg (BNN.ca) on the internet. I now also subscribe to cable TV for BNN and get Fox Business for U.S. exposure. I primarily buy Canadian dividend-paying stocks, with a few exceptions. With U.S. stocks, exchange rates and tax restrictions are baked into the costs – and in some cases I got burned!

Don't try to hit home runs, just go for singles. No matter how well-researched and analyzed a stock recommendation is, remember that the market has a mind of its own. If you buy a good-quality stock, don't sell it if it goes up or down later. Don't buy a lot of the same stock at one time because you may get it cheaper tomorrow. And since stock trades only cost $9.99, just "peck away"; buy a few hundred here and there when the market looks favourable. If you need money, don't sell a stock that's down just to get cash; draw on your emergency fund instead, because the stock may only be temporarily down.

Sometimes the best-laid plans go astray. I'd bought Crescent Point Energy (CPG) at $16 per share many years ago and then sold it to get something better. During the oil boom, when oil hit $100, I re-bought it at $36 per share, mainly for the good annual dividend of $2.78 per share. Thus, I spent $36 to get that $2.78, a 7.7% yield (2.78 divided by 36). Had I kept my original $16 shares, my dividend yield would have been over 17% (2.78 divided by 16). But with oil dropping a few years ago to around $20 a barrel, CPG's share price dropped like a stone, as did their dividend. I hung on until it hit $16, when I pulled the plug and sold it. This meant I incurred a capital loss of about $40,000. But that capital loss was "golden" and helped me avoid future income taxes.

I had acquired Scotiabank (BNS) during the Great Recession of 2008 at $27 and it recovered to $78. So I purposely sold enough BNS for a $40,000 gain exactly equal to my CPG loss; thus cancelling out an unavoidable loss with a deliberate gain – and therefore paying less tax. I did this so that after we croak, our heirs won't be stuck with a big BNS capital gain. After you're gone, CRA deems your entire portfolio to have been liquidated and "sold" on the day you die. That means your estate is liable for capital gains on the "profits". Another lesson I've learned: it's not how much you make, it's how much you can keep after taxes!

When you sell a stock for a loss, you have to wait for 30 calendar days to re-buy it if you want to use the capital loss to off-set your taxes, but you can re-buy for a gain; which I did purposely with BNS (one of our core holdings). And I increased my adjusted cost basis (ACB) for BNS from $27 to $70. I've purposely used BNS selling and re-buying for dividend hopping, which I describe in a later chapter.

I used to have two diversified income funds – Enervest and Sentry Select – that were diversified closed-end funds and holdovers from the income trust era. Closed-end funds are really stocks. They issue a limited number of shares and you must find a seller on the stock exchange if you want to buy them; unlike open-ended mutual funds, where they just issue new units. This gives the fund manager more flexibility; he doesn't need to sell when he doesn't want to, just because somebody wants to redeem your units. Their dividend distributions were both about 12% and their stock prices moved in tandem. So if I needed to generate a loss to off-set a gain elsewhere, I would sell one when it was down and immediately buy the other – which was also down – so I wouldn't miss any monthly distribution income. Sentry Select became an open-ended regular mutual fund and reduced their payouts, so I started to accumulate Enervest exclusively.

Enervest was taken over by Canoe Financial (chairman is Brent Wilson, of Shark Tank fame) and is called the EIT Income Fund (EIT.UN) now. The annual yield is $1.20 and their share price (August 6, 2020) is $9.25 – giving a yield of 13%. It's our largest holding and greatest monthly dividend income generator from both of our TFSAs and NRAs. We've had it off and on since 2003. I'll talk more about EIT.UN in later chapters.

In our NRAs we also have diversified income stock funds in a Canadian bank, a Canadian bank covered-call index, some pipelines, real estate services and a few smaller stocks; see Chapter 12. But first, in Chapter 8, I'll show you a method I've devised to grow your TFSA without using any new money by compounding your annual TFSA contributions.

Chapter 8

COMPOUNDING TFSA CONTRIBUTIONS BY DIVIDEND SWAPPING

With the advent of the TFSA, introduced by the Conservative government in 2009, the whole ballgame changed. Initially you could contribute $5,000 a year of after-tax money (say, from your salary) into a TFSA and any gain (say, from bank interest) was tax-free. That annual contribution got as high as $10,000 before the Liberals capped it at $6,000. If you withdrew money during any year, the next year you could add that amount to your new $6,000 contribution. Now we all have another pension savings vehicle in addition to our NRAs and RSP/RIFs to save for retirement.

In 2011, I thought, why put cash in your TFSA – the prevailing recommendation, generating just 1% interest tax-free – but instead, use high-paying dividend stocks generating 6–13% in dividends? And to beef up your next year's contribution rate of $6,000, why not take out those dividends from the TFSA this year, and put them into a high-interest savings account (Tangerine, maybe) earning 1.5% and pay the tax on that, which would be trivial compared to dividends yielding an average of 8%? So if you generated, say, $10,000 in dividends in your

TFSA this year, took it out and put it into your 1.5% emergency cash account, the next year you could contribute $16,000. But rather than using "new money", i.e. after-tax cash, do it with existing dividend-paying stocks "in kind" from your NRA.

In essence it's swapping stocks from a taxable pocket to another pocket that's tax-free. It's like the concept of compound interest, where each year you'd get interest generated on last year's interest. Here, your TFSA generates more dividend money from the additional dividend stocks transferred from your taxable NRA the previous year. This compounding concept was unique in 2011 when I started it. I've followed this strategy each year and I now generate more dividend income in our TFSAs (15.4%) than in our NRAs (12.6%). If we live long enough, **all our dividends will be tax-free!**

But I didn't stop there. Once I had accumulated enough cash in my emergency fund from these TFSA withdrawals, I started to take low-paying dividend stocks from our TFSAs that were yielding maybe 4% each year and replaced them with higher-yielding NRA stocks, at say 13%, as my contribution the following year. For example, I might take out BNS (paying 5%) in early December from my TFSA and contribute EIT.UN (paying 13%) in kind; plus the new $6,000 contribution in early January the following year.

But care must be taken; when I transferred EIT.UN from my NRA to my TFSA, I had to declare any gain I'd made on EIT.UN while it was in my NRA. If I wanted to retain any loss I'd incurred on EIT.UN, I would have to sell it first in my NRA and transfer the cash to my TFSA instead. Then after 30 days I could use the cash to re-buy EIT.UN in my TFSA.

Once I have all my NRA stocks in our TFSA, I must use "new" money for any further TFSA contributions. But if the inflation rate rises, Tangerine may increase their interest rates. If my taxes on that interest become onerous compared to what I'd pay on dividend stocks, I could reverse this process. Thus, I'd start to transfer stocks from my TFSA into my NRA and replace my TFSA contribution room with cash from my Tangerine emergency fund. That TFSA cash could then be used to either buy stocks or to be saved as cash in a TFSA high-interest savings account such as TD Investment Savings Account TDB8150. In this way I can counter inflation and continue generating my dividends in a tax-favourable mode.

To speed up this process even further, I would withdraw TFSA stocks that had appreciated in value since I first contributed them, thus allowing me to take advantage of tax-free capital gains and at the same time increasing the amount I can contribute the following year. But now I've lost the ability to purposely create a loss to off-set other gains by selling stock at a loss, as I described earlier. My bankrupt Lightstream energy stock still sits in my TFSA and is a $6,000 dead loss! The lesson learned here is to only put quality stocks in your TFSA. But you win some and you lose some!

Could an expert investor analyze and determine if this or other strategies could work for you? Would financial advisors actually do this? Their time would also become pricey to monitor strategies like this, and they would need access to all

Don't Go for Home Runs, Singles Will Do

your investment and savings accounts. Vigilant oversight and careful paperwork is required if you decide to pursue these strategies and only you have a stake in the process – after all, it's your money. Would you want to relinquish control of your investments and savings? However, it's not hard to keep track of these things using the spreadsheet concepts I have developed to monitor my **net worth** and **annual income**, which I describe in the next chapter. You could replicate these spreadsheets, or you could use the information provided by TDW on their trading platform. It's up to you!

Chapter 9

TRACKING NET WORTH AND PREDICTING ANNUAL INCOME

As I have mentioned, I have two spreadsheets: #1 predicts our annual income for tax planning and #2 keeps track of "what we're worth".

No income tax is taken off at source from our pensions or dividends, so we might have to make quarterly installment payments. If you owe more than $3,000 in taxes you **must** pay quarterly, otherwise it's optional. So spreadsheet #1 is used to determine how much we'll make during the year and how much tax we will owe. It lists the stocks we own, how many shares we hold and the amounts of the dividends we'll derive from them. All sources of income are included: taxable dividends, TFSA dividends, expected interest and capital gains, government and work pensions, RIF payments and expected U.S. exchange rates. If our income is appreciably different from the previous year, I can decide if I will need to make quarterly payments and how much they will be.

Spreadsheet #1 also indicates what would happen if one of us passes on. For example, OAS, CPP, U.S. Social Security and work pensions would all change and the survivor's tax load would be higher. I've got ballpark estimates for this. I've also computed which stocks contribute the most to our annual income, both in our TFSAs and our taxable NRAs.

To provide for paying for taxes, I automatically transfer money from my CIBC checking account into a Tangerine "Tax" account – you can use words instead of numbers to describe an account – to draw on to pay quarterly installments or annually as required. Hey, if it's not needed, why give the government the use of my money during the year? I'll get the interest on it now and pay them later if I have to.

I also have the CIBC move over an amount each month to cover all our insurance policies (life, car and house) so I can pay them from Tangerine when they become due. Since we have no dental coverage I'm "self-insured": I automatically transfer a set monthly amount from CIBC to a separate Tangerine "Dental" account to pay any future dental or denture charges. It's like paying for a dental insurance policy, but I get to keep the money if it's not needed. I'm way ahead of the game and sometimes rob it to buy stocks!

I use Ufile (ufile.ca) to do our taxes: I just enter the information from our T3, T5 and T4RIF slips, the capital gains and/or losses provided by TDW, charitable donations and health costs and it determines the best pension split and who should claim the charity and medical tax credits. TD Waterhouse generates most of the information I need for free and Ufile's charge is about $29 for the two of us and they file online; refunds are in less than two weeks. It's a great program. The CRA's assessments usually match Ufile's to the penny. It's in everybody's interest to do their own taxes; that way you can see how much you're paying on different forms of income, such as employment, interest and dividends.

Spreadsheet #2 is for our **net worth**; periodically, I enter the stock prices and emergency cash fund balances and it computes the accrued interest to that date on the GICs in our RIFs, how much money we have in stocks in NRAs and TFSAs, how much each stock is up or down from when I bought it and how much in total we have in equities, RSPs and annuities. I also keep track of how much our net worth has increased since I first started investing. Also included is a 12-month rolling average of our normal living expenses, which is used in spreadsheet #1 as well.

As I've said, I never sell our stocks just because they are up or down and just keep the core stocks "forever" – or at least until my forever! I might shuffle the chairs periodically but I don't sell without a good reason. Dividend hopping is an example of chair shuffling – more of this in a later chapter.

Since I started DIY investing after our GICs matured, our annual net worth has grown over time (see Figure 1).

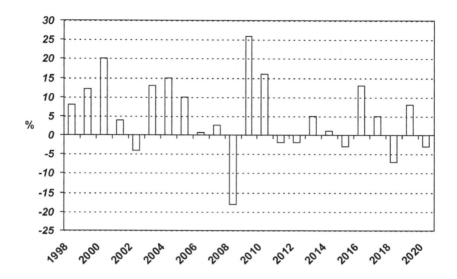

Figure 1: Net worth gain/loss from
DIY investing, 1998 to 2020

That's a simple average 5.5% increase per year spanning a period that has included the dot-com bubble, the Great Recession of 2008, the oil collapse in the mid-teens and the COVID-19 pandemic. Not too shabby, considering we've lived off our net worth extensively all those years as well. As you can see, after each drop in value our net worth has increased in the following years – the market does "always" recover.

Our current net worth (excluding our house) is **44.3%** stocks, **4.6%** annuities and the rest either as GICs or emergency **cash**. Our stock holdings (equities) are down 9.2% overall from what I'd paid for them, but I don't care; they're "just" dividend generators.

To update both spreadsheets takes maybe an hour, which I do two or three times a year. On a daily basis I scan my portfolio Watchlist on the Yahoo Finance website to see what my stocks are doing. You can create your own account and add the stock ticker symbols of your holdings to your own Watchlist. I also scan BNN.ca and the Fox Business website for stock market news.

We're in our spending mode of life; over the past decade we've bought three new cars (five since I've retired), replaced many household appliances and made renovations to our home – even a stair-lift to help go up and down the stairs. We only buy quality items so they'll last. We live well and most market setbacks are easy to handle. All of the new car purchases have been for cash; I make sure to save the money first.

Chapter 10 discusses dividend hopping and bank hopping to beef up the money generated from our NRAs.

Chapter 10

BEEFING UP INCOME BY
DIVIDEND AND BANK HOPPING

Dividend hopping

Companies with dividend-paying stocks announce their ex-dates ahead of actually issuing that dividend. You must own a stock on its ex-date to get the dividend, which is paid out later that month. Since companies pay dividends at different times, why not buy stock in those companies before their ex-date to collect the dividends, and then sell after the ex-date and buy another stock before their ex-date to collect theirs too?

For example, BNS announced the ex-date for their month-end dividend on April 6 and paid it to me on April 30. So if I held BNS at market opening on April 1, I'd get their dividend later that month. I sold BNS on May 7, ensuring a nice big capital loss; remember I'd purposely increased my BNS cost price earlier. Using those proceeds, I immediately bought GWO when it was low too. GWO's ex-date was June 1. I sold GWO on June 11, getting a capital gain. With GWO sale proceeds, I immediately bought EIT.UN. I sold EIT.UN on June 22 after its ex-date of June 15 – with a small capital gain – and with that money re-bought BNS before its new ex-date of July 6. And I got 5% more BNS shares than I'd originally sold. I'd picked up a capital loss on BNS – after ensuring the 30-day wait period for re-buys – and I made a reasonable gain on GWO and a small gain on EIT.UN. I'd also picked up extra dividends (from GWO and EIT.UN) while still maintaining my regular BNS quarterly dividends. I also picked up a "nice" loss overall on BNS sells and re-buys – even after I'd subtracted the gains made on GWO and EIT.UN. Plus, I ended up with more shares of BNS as extra capital. And, over the course of less than a month I made in the region of $4,500. Capital losses can be carried forward to use at your discretion or can be applied against gains from your previous three tax years.

So to review: BNS ex-date was April 1, GWO was June 1 and EIT.UN was mid-June; and this is replicated every quarter. You have a window to hop in and out at opportune times (market up or down) to pick up extra dividends. There's some risk involved. I might have ended up with fewer shares of BNS, not more. In that case, I'd just remain in either GWO or EIT.UN and continue to get their regular dividends. As long as the stock you're going into is a quality stock with a higher dividend, you can wait it out until the market is in your favour.

Look for similar ex-dates about a month apart with good-quality stocks in case you have to remain part-way in the swapping venture. And in my case it was all based on creating a capital loss on BNS, but eventually that won't be available as my cost price drops; i.e. each re-buy at a lower market level drops my cost price, and I don't want to create a gain. You could do this dividend hopping in your RSP, but you wouldn't have this important NRA loss-creation feature.

And why is it so important? Because taxes on capital gains are at 50% – i.e. 50% of your capital gain is added to your taxable income – and I eliminated that problem by off-setting gains with purposely created losses. In an RSP, you'd eventually have to pay tax on the total gain when withdrawn from your RIF. Also, there's a rumour that the Liberal government is thinking about increasing that 50% to, say, 75%, which will affect everyone who has an NRA. The government needs the money to help "pay" for COVID-19 and their vast spending habits. So I'm cleaning the deck before that happens.

Bank hopping

We have virtual bank accounts at Scotiabank's Tangerine, Canadian Tire Bank (CTB) and CIBC's Simplii to store our emergency money. As interest rates dropped, they have been vying for new customers with high-interest special offers for their accounts. For example, Tangerine just offered 2.8% for four months ending Aug 31, 2020 (on deposits to prearranged existing accounts or deposits to new accounts), compared to their existing rate of 0.5%. CTB's rate was 1.8% and Simplii was at 0.5%. So we moved all our money – leaving enough to keep the accounts open – from CTB and Simplii into Tangerine for the four months. After that expires, we'll just move it to the next best offer or stay with the bank with the highest regular rate. Of course, care must be taken to avoid exceeding a bank's Canadian Deposit Insurance Corporation (CDIC) limit of $100,000.

Bank hopping is easily done via the internet and in my case always goes through my CIBC account. If you have an online checking account with another bank you could do the same. But it does require close scrutiny to verify that all the transfers leave and arrive correctly. For security, we have one tower Personal Computer directly connected to the internet, without WiFi, that is dedicated for money transfers, stock trading and CRA taxes – less likely to get viruses. Income swapping isn't a huge venture – but as I've said, only go for singles, not home runs.

Chapter 11 covers the potentially huge savings that can be made from RSP mortgages.

Chapter 11

RSP MORTGAGES

The strategies shown in Chapters 7 and 8 are not available when all your savings and investments reside in an RSP. You can dividend-hop within an RSP/RIF umbrella, but you must have the cash available there to buy the stock. You can't buy the stock ahead of time and you have two days to make up the cash shortfall in your NRAs.

Once an RSP converts to a RIF (which becomes mandatory by age 71) you have to start taking out a minimum percentage each year. Make sure you have a cash reserve within your RSP/RIF (in a high-interest savings account like TDB8150) to meet your annual RIF payments without having to sell stock. The market might be down and you'd need to sell even more of your stocks to meet your withdrawal commitment.

Unfortunately, RSPs are a tax trap so I'm glad that in the past I couldn't take full advantage of the tax-saving RSP contribution deductions. Thank goodness the decision was taken out of my hands.

RSP mortgages, however, can be considered by some people in certain circumstances. With an RSP mortgage, you finance your entire mortgage from your RSP and re-pay the monthly payments to your RSP as if the mortgage was held by a bank. But all the interest and principal is effectively going back to you, not to the bank. You will need a large down payment and a smaller mortgage, since your RSP will be entirely liquidated to supply the cash to purchase your home. You have to be in that sweet spot: enough RSP money for your entire mortgage. And your RSP must be entirely in cash – any stocks or strip bonds must be sold.

There were only two banks that would administer RSP mortgages when my son used this concept: TD Bank and perhaps Laurentian? Anyway, we went to TD Bank, and of course we were already investing with TD Waterhouse. You must pay upfront for mortgage insurance, an initial set-up fee and pay an annual administration fee (about $225) to TD Bank for all their administrative paperwork. And when you take out the mortgage you can negotiate a mortgage rate that's as high and as long as possible, since all the money's going back to you anyway. Then, you must continue to invest that entire mortgage payment every month to recoup your RSP money.

My son arranged for the stock dividends in his NRA account with TDW (which we dubbed his "Mortgage generator" account) to be swept out monthly into his TD Everyday Savings account. Then TD Bank would withdraw his monthly mortgage payment and sent it to his TDW RSP, where he would reinvest it online. All this was done automatically each month without manual intervention. The only thing he needed to do was make sure he generated sufficient NRA dividends to match his monthly premium. He can also make annual prepayments of up to 15%, using a feature offered by TD – which went into his RSP to reinvest.

42

There are a number of cost/benefit considerations for RSP mortgages. Expenditures are the set-up fee, pre-mortgage (upfront) insurance, the annual administration fees, the trivial RSP reinvestment stock purchase commissions and the loss of whatever value your RSP would have grown to had it not been used. The savings are from the interest that would have been paid to the bank, which is considerable; especially during the early years.

For example, you could assume your original RSP would grow at 4% per year for 25 years. That loss is reduced by assuming your repayments of principal and interest each year would grow over the amortized mortgage period. In my son's case, after subtracting all of the costs from the benefit provided by the interest savings, he should save more than $118,000 over 25 years. Well worth it.

Chapter 12 is the culmination of my DIY investing journey; which stocks I hold and how I actually get the money I spend or save.

Chapter 12

MY PORTFOLIO AND HOW
I GET MY MONEY

I am not qualified to advise or recommending that you buy these stocks; I'm only indicating that we have them as our core holdings. Their yields are as of August 13, 2020 at 1 am.

Portfolio construction: while I won't mention how many shares we have of each stock, I will say that in our NRAs both my wife and I have mostly BNS, ZWB, ENB, EIT.UN and BRE. From left to right, that's about their order of importance in terms of value (number of shares held times the share price).

ZEB and ZWB are both index ETFs of the big-six Canadian banks, administered by Bank of Montreal; ZEB is just an equal-weight basket of the six banks, and ZWB uses covered calls; options that protect against downside collapses by buying puts, but limit upside increases by selling calls. Its dividend is 6.82%. That's higher than the yield from the same basket of bank stocks by ZEB (4.82%), which doesn't use options and relies on the bank's individual dividends. I have only ZWB because of its higher dividend. ENB is Enbridge Pipeline (yield is 7.19%) and BNS is Scotiabank at 6.13%. BRE is Bridgemarq Real Estate Services, whose yield is 10.46%.

In our TFSAs, in order of portfolio value, we have EIT.UN, RBN.UN, PINC, ZWU and ENB. RBN.UN and PINC are closed-end funds similar to EIT.UN while ZWU is BMO's utilities and communications index.

In terms of **dividend creation** in our NRAs, 14% of our dividends come from EIT.UN, 11% from ENB, 10% from BRE and the rest from financially oriented stocks (BNS and ZWB). In our TFSA, 86% comes from EIT.UN and the rest from RBN.UN, ENB and PINC.

While again I can't recommend any stocks, all I can say is that's what we have as our core equities and keep them "forever" – notwithstanding the chair shuffling of creating losses and dividend hopping. I don't sell just because they're up or down.

EIT.UN is very compelling to us for its high dividend. I've had it and been adding to it since maybe 2003 – its inception was in 1997. It's very tax-favourable too. Its distribution in 2018 was about 46% in capital gains (only 50% of which is taxable), 6% in dividends (including the dividend tax credit) and the rest as return of capital (ROC), which is not taxable until you sell it. Even then it only incurs a capital gain of 50%. Thus, from $1,000 in EIT.UN's distributions in 2018, only about $290 had to be added to your taxable income; great for an NRA account. But in our case none of that $1,000 was taxable in our TFSAs. In 2019, almost all of the distribution was as ROC and therefore non-taxable; ROC is shown in box 42 of your T3 tax slip.

I'm a very conservative investor and want a comfortable cushion of emergency cash, just in case. That's why only 44%

of our net worth is in stocks – I don't have enough time left to weather a market crash and wait for it to rebound. Younger folks have a longer horizon and can afford to have a much higher stock percentage. As they say, "everybody is different".

In the old days it was said that 100 minus your age was the maximum percentage of your net worth you should have in equities (stocks). That was the trade-off to account for a market drop and subsequent recovery. By that calculation, at the age of 82 I should only have 18% in stocks. But with the today's low rates, you need more like 100 minus your age squared (divided by 100). Thus I should have 100 minus (82 times 82 divided by 100), or 33%. But I have 44%; not too bad considering the emergency savings cushion I keep.

If you consider following in my footsteps you must be vigilant, but not obsessive; just scan the market every few days to see what you options you might consider. Anybody who thinks paid advisors would do what I've done is fooling themself. They certainly wouldn't spend the time on all their clients to assess whether they should sell/trade to maximize their accounts; maybe the richer ones, but not the little guys. And you'd have to provide access to all your bank records, etc. If you do it yourself and are successful you can feel pretty good; if not, you'll have nobody to blame but yourself. When you're right it's exhilarating. I'm not an expert, but what I know, I know well; I started at the ground floor and was successful. So can you. It's fun!

Chapter 13 reviews the lessons I've learned so you can adopt the good ones and avoid the bad ones.

Chapter 13

THE GOOD AND BAD LESSONS LEARNED ON MY JOURNEY

I hope this book has been interesting and informative. I wrote it as my legacy and to show how other novices can do the same as me. The time spent in "research" – thinking what to do and how to do it – can be done while walking, working out, boating, fishing, etc. That way you're "killing two birds with one stone".

The first lesson I learned was that I can do it. A financial advisor simply wouldn't have the time to analyze and implement each option for your particular situation, as you do. It's not his money, it's yours! You have a bigger stake than he does.

Another lesson is confidence: remember that the stock market always recovers and if you aren't in it when it does, you lose. You'll save a bundle of money by eliminating advisor fees. And you are in control.

Avoid buying mutual funds – normal open-ended funds – because the fees will really erode your investment. Open-ended funds simply buy more units with your investment and sell units when people redeem their units; possibly at the wrong time, when the market's down and more shares will be needed to meet the redemption request. Closed-end funds – such as EIT.UN – avoid this dilemma. My "endorsement" of them is unsolicited; I get nothing from them for it; nor for my praise of TD Direct Investing.

Buy into the market when it's down, not up; but don't buy in all at once, but just a bit at a time. Nobody can buy in right at the bottom or sell right at the top. Don't be concerned that stock might drop after you buy it; or that it'll go up after you sell it! It's just "par for the course". Studies have shown it's not "timing the market" but "time in the market" that's paramount.

Take advantage of what the market "gives you". If it drops, consider using some of the techniques outlined in Chapter 7; creating losses to off-set taxes on gains. If it goes up, smile but don't sell. Treat your stocks as dividend generators, and use your emergency cash as needed.

Only buy quality dividend-paying stocks and hold them "forever". Open an emergency cash fund for drawing out money when it's needed rather than selling good stocks at the wrong time. Don't DRIP, use a discount investing platform like TD's WebBroker to buy new shares with your dividends yourself when the market's favourable (i.e. down). Remember it's only $9.99 per trade.

Try to put your investment savings in after-tax money (NRAs) rather than just in RSPs. As I have shown, this will give you many more options to use. Strongly consider, when conditions are "right", to strategically create capital losses and re-buy an alternative stock so as to not miss any dividends. It's not how much you make, it's how much you can keep away from the government.

Try to maximize your TFSA savings using some of the techniques I have developed. It will vastly increase your contributions beyond the normal $6,000 per year and it requires no "new money" – i.e. from your emergency savings account. And it'll reduce your taxes by shifting your dividend-paying stocks from just being tax-favourable to completely tax-free.

Find out how much it costs you to live by implementing my approach. Also, keep track of your investments in a similar way to me. The spreadsheet development for both net worth and income tracking will sharpen your mind, be informative and might provide an incentive to attempt different options. And you can quantitatively compare each option during one time frame to another to see any improvements, not just rely on a subjective "well, maybe". First do the math to see what you could expect for different options, so you won't be disappointed afterwards – in other words, what-if scenarios.

Every little bit helps: if you save $200 by say moving your savings from one bank to another with minimal work, it's worth it. I come from a generation that routinely made something out of nothing. I used to say "a little bit here, a little bit there and pretty soon you got two bits". In the old days, two bits was a 25 cent coin. Don't try to hit home runs, singles will do it!

Disregard those who say "I don't care what happens in the market, it doesn't affect me". Everybody has a stake in the market; either through work pensions (defined contributions or defined benefits), CPP investments, mutual funds and even GICs issued by banks; which are themselves stocks and subject to market forces. The market is the life blood of our economy and affects our well-being. Treat experts as just another opinion and not as "the" complete solution. You can talk to a dozen knowledgeable experts and get twelve different opinions. Consider them all and make your own decision.

Because of economic reasons and tragic circumstances I only had very modest savings in GICs when I started my DIY investment journey but parlayed them into a mechanism that gave us a comfortable living and financial security. And it kept my mind active.

Afterword

Unfortunately not many people today understand the value of money: how to budget, how much interest they're paying on their credit card, the value of saving regularly and the different savings vehicles that are available. Kids today don't have a clue about these things. They should be taught in elementary school about allowances, the value of money and how it affects their parents. In high school, they should be focused on part-time jobs and learning about budgeting, credit cards and debt, car expenses and maintenance, mortgages and their costs, taxes and about defined benefit vs. defined contribution pensions.

My generation had to make do. When the money wasn't there we didn't go on vacation or get a newer car. My grandparents went through the Depression and my parents spanned both that and the post-war recovery. How they survived amazed me, especially after my dad died and I found out little they had. I'm so glad I paid my entire way through university – except for one time I borrowed $40 from my dad because I'd run out of money while at school; I never did pay it back.

My wife's parents never had a car. My grandfather worked 54 years and got no pension. My generation generally did better than the previous ones, and my sons might do better than I did. But with free trade, jobs are hurting for this up-coming group of kids; no matter what they're promised.

We saved the money needed before we bought something, rather than paying for it over time. The one exception was my mortgage; I paid it down after 11 years in 1978, at the age of 40. Thankfully I did so then, because I was laid off three years later. But I was in the camp of those who knew nothing about mutual funds and investing in stocks and it hampered me when starting my journey. I had never thought about retirement until I "had" to. As I've said previously, sometimes people spend more time planning their vacations than planning their retirement – me included. I was lucky I took the approach I've outlined herein.

I was going to call this book (with tongue in cheek) *I Admire the Wisdom of Those Who Come to Me for Advice*, but it's too long. It's a quote from a Readers Digest article I saw in 1967 and thought was funny and neat. I hope others won't call it *There's Nothing Worse than a Know-It-All, Who Is Sometimes Right*. I wasn't right all the time – nobody is – but just a lot of the time. And I had fun and got a lot of self-satisfaction doing it. And I had to get those two quotes in somewhere.

The best compliment I received while working in industry was "He gets the job done". In teaching, the best was "He made me think". Hopefully I've accomplished both in my third career. Always "think" to help keep your faculties intact. My mind's always thinking. I "never" just watch TV; I read a lot, over 50 books per year. I'm a conservative who believes in capitalism, self-sufficiency and freedom of choice. You shouldn't penalize success and reward failure.

At the end all you have is your integrity. And remember, family and friends are the most important things in life; everything else pales by comparison.

A Glossary of Terms

ACB – Adjusted cost basis (stock cost price)

BNS – Scotiabank (formerly Bank of Nova Scotia)

BRE – Bridgemarq Real Estate Services

CDIC – Canadian Deposit Insurance Corporation

CPG – Crescent Point Energy

CPP – Canada Pension Plan

CRA – Canada Revenue Agency

DIY – Do it yourself

DRIPping – Dividend reinvestment plan

DSC – Deferred sales charge

EIT.UN – Closed-end income fund from Canoe Financial

ENB – Enbridge Pipeline

ETF – Exchange-traded fund, usually tracking a market index

Ex-date – The date you must own a stock to receive its dividend

GWO – Great-West Lifeco

ICT – Income trust

MER – Management expense ratio

NRA – Non-registered account (my own term)

OAS – Old Age Security

PINC – Purpose Multi-Asset closed-end fund

RBN.UN – Blue Ribbon closed-end fund

RIF – Registered Retirement Income Fund, or RRIF (subject to mandatory withdrawals)

ROC – Return of capital

RSP – Registered Retirement Savings Plan, or RRSP

SS – U.S. Social Security

Stock symbols – Ticker symbols for trading stocks

T3, T5, T4RIF – Tax slips for tax filing

TDW – TD Waterhouse, the TD Bank brokerage that provides TD Direct Investing

TFSA – Tax-Free Savings Account

Ufile.ca – Online tax return filing

ZEB – Big-six Canadian bank index

ZWB – Big-six Canadian bank covered-call index

ZWU – Utilities and communications index

CPSIA information can be obtained
at www.ICGtesting.com
Printed in the USA
LVHW091606011120
670390LV00022B/495